TOGETHER

Family stories, poems and prayers
of the Marshall family

Catherine Marshall

TOGETHER WITH GOD

Family stories, poems and prayers
of the Marshall family

HODDER AND STOUGHTON
LONDON SYDNEY AUCKLAND TORONTO

British Library Cataloguing in Publication Data

Together with God : favourite
stories poems and prayers of the Marshall
family.
1. Family——Prayer-books and devotions
I. Marshall, Catherine, 1914–1983
242   BV255

ISBN 0–340–40632–1

Hodder & Stoughton Editorial Office: 47 Bedford Square, London
WC1B 3DP.

The author wishes to express her appreciation to the Estate of Laura E. Richards and to Little, Brown & Company for permission to adapt "The Coming Of The King" from the book THE GOLDEN WINDOWS; to Doubleday & Company, Inc., for permission to adapt for "The Babies Who Wouldn't Eat", twenty-six lines from PEACE IN THE HEART by Archibald Rutledge; to Angelo Patri and to *Young Wings*, the magazine of the Junior Literary Guild, for permission to reprint "The Little Red Wagon"; to Harper & Row for permission to use one sentence from YOUR CHILD AND GOD by Robbie Trent; to Canon Wallace Elliott, for Peter Marshall's adaptation of his benediction; to Grace Hildebrand, Elizabeth Ann Campagna, and Leonora W. Wood for many helpful suggestions; to her two youngest and best critics — Mickey Campagna and Tommy Wharton. "The King with Wet Feet" is based on an English legend, and "The Way of a Crab" on a tale from Aesop. The author wishes to express her appreciation also to the Estate of Heywood Hale Broun and to Doubleday & Company, Inc., for permission to use "The Toy Dog", adapted from "Frankincense and Myrrh", reprinted by permission of the copyright owners; for "Bradley Does His Sums", adapted from CHILDREN'S STORY SERMONS by Hugh T. Kerr, published by the Fleming H. Revell Company; for "The Latchstring Was Out", adapted from THE FRIENDLY STORY CARAVAN, collected by a Committee of the Philadelphia Yearly Meeting of Friends, Anna Pettit Broomell, Chairman, Copyright 1935, 1948, 1949 by Anna Pettit Broomell, published by J. B. Lippincott Company, used by permission; for "Buying His Own", adapted from "The Story of the Lost Sail Boat", by Jacob J. Sessler, from JUNIOR SERMON STORIES, published by Fleming H. Revell Company; to Elizabeth Anne Campagna for permission to print her "I Knew God Was There"; to Mr. Joseph Allen for his invaluable help in research work in the Library of

Congress; to my secretary, Margaret Bradley Giles, for her steady support and help. "There Is Gladness Everywhere", by Margaret E. Sangster was published by Harper & Brothers; "Solomon and the Bees" is based on an old legend taken from the Midrash; "The Easter Flower" is based on an Oriental legend; "Big Shot — the Little Sunfish", is an adaptation of a story by Worthington Stewart.

If there should remain any unacknowledged material in this book, the publisher will welcome word to that effect and will give proper credit in all future editions.

CONTENTS

COME IN — WON'T YOU?

In our home, it has been the custom to have family prayers in the evening right after dinner. Even before the dinner dishes were washed, the whole family would gather in our living room.

"Get comfortable now," Peter John's daddy would say. To Peter John, comfortable meant sitting on a little stool, or lying propped on his elbows on the rug before the open fire. To Jeff, our cocker spaniel, comfortable meant lying contentedly at his master's feet.

Peter-daddy, seated in his big easy chair, would read a bit from the Bible lying open on his knees. Then often he would tell us a story. These stories helped us to understand what God is like and how He wants us to act, so that we may please Him and become His happy, helpful children.

This nicest-time-of-the-whole-day then would be closed with prayer. Peter John's father often told him, "Just talk to God about anything on your mind, Peter John, in your own language, in your own way. That's what prayer is."

We thought you would like our family-prayertime stories as much as we like them. That's why Peter John and I decided to make this book. We have included a few of the talking-things-over sort of prayers too.

As you look at and read this book, we hope that you will feel that you are a guest in our home. Friendship is here — and God's love.

Come in — won't you?

THE LITTLE
RED WAGON

In a Western town, there was a little mission church, where the true Christmas spirit still lived. It was the custom there, on Christmas Eve, to put many candles on the altar and, close by, little figures of the Nativity scene. There was the manger in the stable, and Mary and Joseph, the Baby Jesus lying in the straw, and the animals in their stalls. And overhead was the one bright star which guided the Wise Men to Bethlehem.

Early one Christmas morning, the pastor of the church went to see that all the little figures were in place for the first service. He was horrified to see that the tiny figure of the Baby Jesus was gone. The pastor looked everywhere, but he could not find it.
As the pastor left the church, he was almost run over by a little boy racing a red wagon along the pavement.

It was Pierre — the baker's son. The pastor smiled and started to speak to the boy, when, suddenly, he noticed in the red wagon, the missing figure of the Christ Child.

"Pierre!" he cried. "It was *you!* You took the Baby Jesus. Why did you do it?"

Pierre hung his head and was silent. The pastor scolded and questioned. Still Pierre would not explain. He just hung his head and dug the toe of one scuffed shoe into the side of the other.

"It — it was like this," Pierre finally blurted out, "I — I wanted a red wagon for Christmas, and I prayed. I asked Jesus to let me have a red wagon. And — and I promised Him that if I got one, I'd give Him a ride in it. It's His birthday, you know."

The good pastor smiled down at the little boy, and there were tears in his eyes.

"I'm sorry I scolded, Pierre. I didn't understand. You are quite right. It *is* His birthday, and you have given Him the nicest gift of all."

THANK YOU, GOD, FOR LITTLE THINGS

Things I like best
are little things,
Like baby birds
and fluffy chicks,
the puppies down the street;
A shiny rock,
My little jeep,
The buttercups we pick;
A baby calf,
Some kittens,
Our playhouse just so big.
Jesus, You were little once,
You know how it is.

GRACE BEFORE MEALS

For colours in the food we eat,
For smells that smell so good,
For things to taste and things to see,
For Mummy and Daddy
And for Thee,
Father in Heaven, we thank Thee.

Amen

THOUGHTS

I want to do
What I want,
But then I find
I don't always like
what I want.
I guess, God,
You'd better
straighten me
out.

THE BABIES WHO WOULDN'T EAT

Once a man who lived down South captured a family of five baby raccoons. He gave them plenty of food, but for days they would not eat.

To keep their pen dry, the man put their pan of water just outside the cage. The only way the little raccoons could get to the water was through a small hole in the wire. But the food on the floor of the pen lay untouched. Lumps of sugar were added to the food to tempt their appetites. Still the babies would not eat. Days passed. Their little sides were caved in with hunger.

The man was kindhearted, and he was troubled about the hungry babies. What could be wrong? Were the baby raccoons pining for their mother?

One morning he went early to the pen. As he got there, he saw one of the little raccoons pick up a lump of sugar and head for the water bowl. The raccoon pushed the sugar through the wire into the water; then he tried to put the other paw through to wash the sugar, but the hole was not large enough.

Suddenly the man knew why the babies hadn't been eating. They had simply been heeding their mother! All raccoons are taught to wash their food before eating it. The baby raccoons were ready to starve, rather than disobey.

The man rushed for a pan of water to see if he was right. This time he put it down in the middle of the pen. Right away, all five little raccoons picked up some food, headed straight for the water, washed the food thoroughly, and ate it happily.

Human children, you see, are not the only ones who have to learn to obey. Obedience is something God requires of every one of us.

THE KING
WITH WET FEET

King Canute of England lived in much splendour. Always he was surrounded by many courtiers and servants. These men thought that they could please the King by praising him.

"You are mighty and powerful," they would say.

"Nothing in all the world would dare to disobey you. Your glory will last for ever. Your kingdoms are safe from any army. You are so great that no one will take a foot of land from you."

Finally, the King grew tired of hearing all of this praise. He was a very wise King, and he knew that what his courtiers were saying just wasn't true. But he listened without saying anything.

Then one day he turned to his servants. "Bring me my great Chair of State," he ordered. When they brought the Chair of State, he said, "Now follow me, all of you, and bring the Chair of State with you."

The courtiers were greatly surprised when King Canute led them straight to the seashore.

The tide was out at the time. The King walked far down the beach, and ordered his chair placed at the very edge of the water, facing the sea. Then he sat down in the chair without saying another word.

Of course everyone around him wondered what he was doing, but no one dared ask the King.

After a while, the tide turned, and a little wave slipped over the sand and washed right over the Royal Feet. The courtiers' feet got wet too.

Then King Canute rose up, and stretching out his hand toward the sea, he called out in a loud and kingly voice, "This land whereon I stand is *mine.* None of the people on this land dare to resist my rule. I command thee, sea, not to mount up on my land, nor wet my feet. I command thee to retreat right away."

Just as he finished saying this, another wave — this time a big one — came hissing and foaming up the beach. This wave not only wet the Royal Feet but the Royal Ankles as well. The water poured over the

legs of the courtiers who were standing around the throne and did not dare back out of the way.

Then Canute rose again. "Let all the people on earth know," he said solemnly, "that kings have no power that God does not give them. The power of kings is vain. No one is worthy of the name of King except Him who made the land and the sea, and whose Word is the law of heaven and earth."

Then King Canute and his wet courtiers walked silently back to the town. After that no one dared to praise the King for his power and glory.

The town of Southampton, England, has been built on the very spot where this took place. There, on the wall of a little house near the docks, I have seen a small bronze plaque on which are these words:

On this spot
in 1032
King Canute rebuked
his courtiers.

GOD LOVES YOU

Said the sparrow to the robin, "I
    should really like to know
Why these anxious human beings
    rush about and worry so."
Said the robin to the sparrow, "I
    think that it must be
That they have no Heavenly Father
    such as cares for you and me."

ELIZABETH CHENEY

MANNERS

I'd be as impolite a child
As impolite could be,
To eat and quite forget to say
A thank-you, Lord, to Thee.

HAPPY EASTER!

The sun rose in a soft pink glow over the garden of Joseph of Arimathaea. Sleepy birds shook themselves awake and began to flutter and twitter. A white rabbit peered out from behind the trunk of a great tree. A dappled baby deer nuzzled her mother awake. A black sheep munched on the dew-drenched grass.

But this sunrise — so long ago — was different from any other in the world's history, for this was the dawning of the first Easter.

On Friday, Jesus had been taken down from the Cross — dead. Sorrowfully and gently, His friends had laid Him in a cave in Joseph's garden.

Now — on Easter Sunday morning — there were strange stirrings within the cave. And soon, out into the rose-tinted sunrise, walked Jesus — alive.

All the animals in the garden saw Him. Long before, at Jesus's birth, the friendly animals in the stable had been the first to welcome Him. So once again they welcomed Him, even before His human friends.

A dove settled on His shoulder and cooed her delight. The white rabbit scampered joyously around His feet. The little deer nestled close, and He smiled and stroked her dappled head. Birds circled His head, singing their happiest songs. The black sheep lay down at His feet.

Perhaps that is why the animals still help us celebrate Easter. The hen gives us her eggs to dye in rainbow colours. Fluffy yellow chickens appear in children's Easter baskets. Live bunnies with pink eyes, toy bunnies, and Easter eggs decorate the store windows.

And out on green hillsides, frisky lambs run joyously. Baby horses stand on tall, uncertain legs. Trees burst into bloom, and birds build their nests and sing happily. Each animal is saying in its own way, "We are happy because spring is here again, and love and beauty have come to earth." And because Jesus rose from the dead on that first Easter, we too are happy, for not one of us need ever be lonely or afraid again. Happy Easter!

PRAYER
FOR A SICK DOG

Dear Jesus, this is Johnny again
sending You another call for help;
I'm up in my cherry-tree house.
You seem closer up here in the sky
with green leaves and birds all around.

It's like this — my dog, Jeff, is sick.
Mummy and I have read in the Bible
about how You love little lambs,
because You're the Good Shepherd,
and about how You found the one
        lost lamb
and carried him home in Your arms
and made him well.

So we know You'll be sorry about Jeff,
        too.
Jeff doesn't want to run and play now.
His droopy ears droop more than ever.
He just looks at me with sad brown eyes
that seem to say, "Johnny, pl-ea-se
        help me."
So, dear Jesus, will You be Jeff's doctor?
And will You cure him the way
You did that baby lamb?

If You will, I'll nurse Jeff
and do whatever You say.
Mummy thinks the three of us
can pull him through.

He's a nice spaniel —
even if he does rumple rugs.
Anyway, I love him.
Thank You, Jesus, for listening to me.

Amen

A SMALL BOY TALKS
TO GOD

Dear God — when I was five and
    very young,
I thought all our food
came from grocery shops.
I just couldn't understand why Daddy
kept thanking You.

But now I'm six —
and much, much wiser.
Now I know that shops
would have no food, if it weren't for You,
if You didn't make things grow.

So thank You, God, for funny little seeds
that grow into pods of green peas
and red tomatoes and yellow bananas
and shiny apples.
Thank You for the rain and sunshine
to make the seeds grow.
Thank You for the farmer-men
who plant the seeds,
and for the men who drive big trucks
to take the food to market.

Thank You for shopkeepers like
        Mr. Barnes
in his big white apron,
for Daddy who buys our food,
and for Mummy, who cooks
such good things for us to eat.
Thank You, God.

Amen

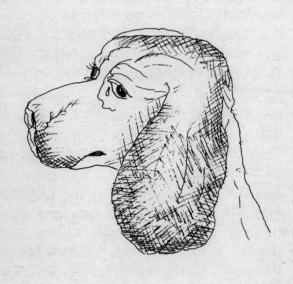

SAVED BY A TAIL

Corky was a little black cocker spaniel. He was not just a make-believe dog, but a real one who lived in Winchester, Massachusetts.

One cold November day, Corky went for a walk. Soon he came to a lake named Winter Pond. The cold weather had covered Winter Pond with a thin layer of ice.

Corky walked out on the ice. But when he had reached the middle of the pond, the ice broke, and the little black dog fell into the cold water.

The little spaniel started crying and barking. Many people heard him and came running to Winter Pond. All of them wanted to rescue Corky, but they knew if they walked out on the thin ice, they, too, would fall in.

Still, Corky cried, and a big English setter heard his cries. This big dog was Corky's best friend. The big English setter raced to the edge of Winter Pond. While all the people watched, he started inching his way out on the thin ice. Very gently he put his big feet down, so the ice would not break under him.

Finally, the big dog reached Corky. He put his mouth close to Corky's ear, to tell him something important in dog-language. It must have been his plan for rescuing the little spaniel.

Then slowly, very slowly, the big dog turned around, until his long tail was right in front of the little dog's face. Corky sank his teeth in his friend's tail. When he had a firm hold, his friend began crawling towards shore. Corky hung on for dear life and was soon pulled out of the icy water. Jesus said, "Be ye kind, one to another." The big English setter knew how to be kind. He rushed to help his friend Corky when the little dog needed help. Do you watch for ways to help?

THE
BENEDICTION

And now may Almighty God
in His mercy and in His love,
Bless all those who are
near and dear to us,
In our work by day
and in our homes by night.
And keep us all in His peace
through Jesus Christ our Lord.

Amen

CUB SCOUT'S PRAYER

Dear Father, this is Johnny talking.
Of course You know
I'm at camp.
I've tried to be good today —
and I really have had a good time.
Swimming and paddling that canoe,
and going fishing were all such fun.
I'm glad You thought
        of making cool blue water
and sunshine and silvery fish.
But, God, what about that fish
that got away?
Where did he go?
You made such pretty things, God.
I like the way the willow trees
hang over the lake.
When we paddled
        our canoe through them,
it was like being in a small green house.

I like the red of the butterfly's wings,
the funny feel
        of the dandelion flower I picked,
the big gold moon tonight,
and the feel of wiggling my toes
in the cool wet sand.
Thank You, God,
for making all these things.

Oh — and please bless Mother and Dad —
and help me to be a good scout
        tomorrow.
Good night, God.

Amen

PRAYER
FOR FORGIVENESS

Today I found my toy telephone
and I telephoned to God.
I said, "Hello, God —
are You there? How are You?
This is Johnny talking.
I want to tell You I'm sorry —
sorry about the way I acted
        this morning.
Something got into me.
It was like lions and tigers on the inside,
I'm not happy when I'm bad.

"I'm sorry for being cross to Mummy,
sorry for yelling 'no' in a scratchy voice
and banging the kitchen door.
Sorry for forgetting to feed Jeff
so that Jeff had to go away hungry.
Sorry for being mean to Betty —
She said I had a fussy forehead,
and I grabbed away my fire engine
and hurt her foot.
I *am* sorry.

"Daddy says the minute —
the very minute — I'm truly sorry,
and tell You what I've done wrong,
You'll forgive me.

"But I think You'd like it too,
if I tell Mummy and Betty
and Jeff that I'm sorry.
So I'll do that right now.
Then everything will be all straight again.
Good-bye — and thank You, God.

Amen."

WORRY BIRDS

Lots of people pray. Then, when they have stopped praying, they keep right on worrying. But that isn't real prayer. Worry and prayer just don't mix together. Do you know why?

Suppose a boy has a broken bicycle. He takes it to a bicycle shop and asks the repairman to fix it.

The man says, "Yes, I'll fix your bike. Leave it with me. You can pick it up tomorrow afternoon."

So the boy leaves his bike and goes home. But suppose that same afternoon, the boy starts worrying. Somehow, he doesn't trust the repairman to fix his bike. What if the boy gets it into his head that the man can't do the job well? What if the boy should actually rush back to the shop and take his broken bike home, before the man has even had a chance to work on it? That would be foolish, wouldn't it? Yet, that's the way a lot of us treat God.

We ask him to fix something in our lives, or to give us something that we need very much. Then, like the little boy, we start worrying. We doubt that God can fix it. And we actually take our problem back, before He has had a chance to work on it. Worry and prayer do not go together. If you want God to fix something for you, you must trust Him. Try to trust God at least as much as you would the bicycle repairman.

THE WAY
OF A CRAB

The tide had gone out, and two crabs were strolling about on the beach.

Suddenly, one crab cried out to the other, "I don't like the way you walk. You sway from side to side. It doesn't look nice. Why don't you just walk straight forward?"

"Well," replied the other crab, "you walk straight yourself. Show me what you mean, and I'll walk just as you do."

But, as everyone knows, a crab cannot walk straight. Crabs are made so that they have to waddle from side to side.

It's a strange thing that the faults we see most clearly in other people are often the faults we have ourselves.

That's one reason why we should not find fault with other people. Don't tell anyone else to walk straight, unless you can walk straight yourself.

THEIR FACES FELL

Two workmen were fixing the roof of a house. They slipped and fell down a large chimney, landing on the floor below.

Both men scrambled to their feet, unhurt. But in the process of falling, one man had got black soot all over his face. The other man had put one arm over his face as he fell, so that his face was perfectly clean.

Now before the two men went back to work, the man with the clean face went and washed; the man with the sooty face went back to work without washing.

Can you explain why they did that?

This is a test to see how well you can think; but it is quite easy.

You see, the workmen looked at each other. The man with the clean face looked at the black face of his friend and assumed that his was sooty too.

The man with the black face saw the clean face of the other and assumed that his was clean.

Both men were wrong because they were judging themselves by each other. That is never a safe thing to do. There is only one true standard for us to judge ourselves by. That is the perfect standard we have in Jesus.

THE GARDEN BEYOND THE GATE

Once a little boy named Andrew lived in a tiny stone cottage in the village of Dunfermline in Scotland. Andrew's father was a weaver. The family was very poor, but the tiny cottage was as clean as could be, and the bit of a garden was filled with bright flowers.

Every day on the way to school, Andrew passed some tall iron gates. He would often stop and look through the iron grillwork. Beyond, there was a great house surrounded by rolling green lawns and beautiful gardens. And out beyond the house there was a little valley, called Pittencrieff Glen, through which a singing stream wound its way.

But the gates were always closed, and the little boy could never go in.

"When I grow up, if I make a lot of money," Andrew often said to himself, "I'll buy that beautiful park. Then I'll open the gates wide and invite all the children in the town to play inside. When I own it, the gates will never be locked again."

When he was thirteen, Andrew's family sold everything they owned in Scotland and moved to America. They went to Pittsburgh. There young Andrew started to work as a bobbin boy in a cotton factory. He didn't earn much, but it was not long before he was earning more.

Indeed, Andrew seemed to have been given the gift of knowing how to make money. As the years went by he became very rich.

When some people get a great deal of money, they want to keep all of it for themselves. But Andrew found that it was fun to share.

So he built libraries and concert halls; he gave parks and organs; he gave money to colleges and universities. He gave away money to work towards peace and to reward men for acts of courage and bravery.

In the year 1868, Andrew and his mother went back to Scotland on a visit. Andrew had not forgotten about that little boy peering through the tall iron gates, nor had he forgotten the promises he had made to himself. He had seen many beautiful places in the world, but the park behind the iron gates in his own town in Scotland still seemed the most beautiful of all.

So he bought it, and right away he opened the gates and gave the park to the people of Dunfermline. Ever after the children have run and laughed and played in Andrew Carnegie's beautiful park. And each year — in August — when flowers are at their loveliest, all the school children have a picnic there. Not a single one is left out.

THE COMING OF THE KING

One day a long time ago, some children were playing in their playground, when a herald rode through the town, blowing a trumpet and shouting, "The King! The King will pass along this road today. Make ready for the King!"

The children stopped playing and looked at one another. "Did you hear that?" one asked.

"The King is coming," said another. "He might look over the wall and see our playground. It's messy. We must make it all nice and neat for him."

The playground was indeed messy. Broken toys lay all around. There were scraps of paper on the ground. The children had a lot of work to do before it was tidied and looked really neat again.

"Now it looks better," one child said. "But kings are used to such fine things. Let's make it pretty."

So the children gathered green, sweet-smelling branches and scattered them on the ground. They brought leaves and fresh ferns and hung them on the wall. One little boy picked marigolds and threw them on the ground. "To make it look like gold," he said.

When they had finished, the playground looked so beautiful that the children just stood and looked at it.

"Let's keep it like this always," one said, clapping her hands with delight.

"Yes, that's just what we'll do," everyone shouted.

The children waited all day for the coming of the King, but he didn't come. Towards evening, though, just as the sun was setting, an old man with travel-worn clothes and a kind, tired face passed along the road and stopped to look over the wall.

"What a pretty place," the old man said.

"May I come in and rest?"

"Oh, yes," the children said. So they brought him in and helped him to a seat they had made of an old barrel. They had covered the barrel with a red cloak to make it look like a throne. It made a fine throne.

"This is our playground," one little boy said. "We made it all pretty for the King, but he never came. But we are going to keep it pretty always in case he does come."

The gentle old man sat and rested. He smiled at the children with such kind eyes that they gathered around him and told him their best secrets — about the five puppies in the barn, about the tree where the robin's nest with the blue eggs was, and about the seashore where the golden shells grew. And the man nodded and understood it all.

After a while, the man asked for a cup of cool water, so the children brought it to him in their best, clean tin cup. They were very kind to the stranger.

Then the old man thanked the children and rose to go. But before he left, he laid his hands on their heads, and each child felt a warm thrill as he did so.

The children stood by the wall and waved to him as he went slowly down the road.

The sun was setting, and the golden light fell in long slanting rays across the road.

"He looked so tired," said one of them.

"But he was so nice," said another.

"See," said the smallest child, "see how the sun shines on his hair! It looks like a golden crown."

Maybe — maybe the man was the King after all.

Now King Jesus has come to earth. And He has promised us, "Lo, I am with you always. ..."

We can't see Him with our eyes, but we can feel His presence in our hearts. Do you try to make your work and play fine enough to please the King?

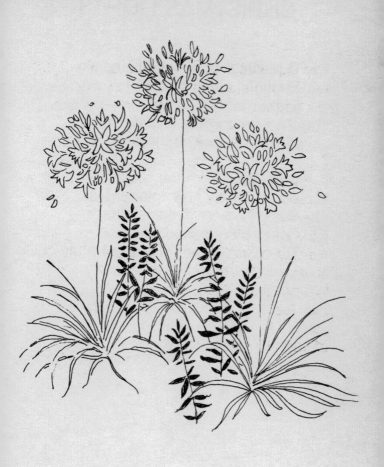

CHRISTMAS LIGHTS

O starlight from the singing sky,
Starlight, come to earth!
Blazon every fragrant tree,
Shine in children's eyes, that we
May kneel to love the Baby King.

O starlight from the singing sky,
Come swiftly now to earth!
Shine in every darkened place,
Capture every land and race,
Till children everywhere can bring
Happy gifts to praise the King.

MORNING

The stars are gone,
The silver moon is hiding
from the sun.
A merry bird
just called to me,
"Wake up, the day's begun."
Good morning, World!
Good morning, God!

NIGHT

Tonight the earth
is crowned with stars,
a soft wind hums a tune,
And for a hat
the pine tree wears
a slice of saucy moon.
Good night, World!
Good night, God!

JESUS IS
OUR FRIEND

We like to share happy times in our home with our friends. One day a group of Peter John's friends were playing Pirate Treasure Hunt. This was an exciting game. But it was a hard game for Tim, who was only four. Tim said, "My Friend Jesus will help me find the treasure."

Tim's older brother, David, was scornful. "That's a silly thing to say, Tim. You don't talk about the Lord Jesus that way. You just pray about important things, not everyday things."

After the game was finished, the children were sitting in front of the open fire looking at their treasures. David laughingly told of Tim's talking to his Friend Jesus about the Treasure Hunt.

I said, "I know what you mean, David. But Tim's feeling is right, you know. Jesus does want to be our Friend. He told us so Himself."

"He did! Where?"

"Right in the fifteenth chapter of John. He really said it clearly, HENCEFORTH I CALL YOU NOT SERVANTS ... BUT I

HAVE CALLED YOU FRIENDS ... You know how we like to be with our friends often. Well, Jesus wants to be our Friend every day, not just on Sundays. And that, I think, is what Tim had in mind. He was certain that the Lord Jesus was here today with us in our fun."

After that, David and Peter John and the other children had so many adventures in learning to be God's friends, that they suggested that I tell you about some of them. That is why I decided to make this book. I hope that you too will decide that you want the fun of being FRIENDS WITH GOD.

THE
EASTER FLOWER

When Jesus was a baby, His Mother Mary had to flee with Him to keep Him from being killed by the cruel King Herod. Joseph and Mary and the Baby crossed the hot plains of Jericho.

When Mary alighted from the ass on which she was riding, a little flower sprang up at her feet. It was as if the little flower wanted to greet the infant Saviour whom she carried in her arms.

These little yellow flowers sprang up at all the places where the Baby Jesus rested. And as He grew up, wherever He ran and played, there were the little flowers. He called them "Roses of Jericho".

Then came that sad day when He died on the cross. On that day all the little flowers withered and faded. But three days later, Jesus walked out of the tomb in which His friends had gently laid Him — alive for evermore. And as He walked out into the rose-tinted sunrise of that first Easter morning, the little Rose of Jericho sprang to life to greet Him. The little flowers began blooming gaily all over the land as a symbol of the joy in the earth, because Christ was risen.

That is why all of us are so happy at Easter. Flowers bloom in the fields and in our gardens just as did the Roses of Jericho. Some of the trees burst into bloom. Birds joyously build their nests. Little girls wear flowers on their hats. Children dye eggs bright colours and laugh and sing. They are happy, not just because spring has come, but because they have a living Saviour to love. They know that Jesus will always be with them, to be their Friend and to help them.

That is the real meaning of Easter.

GRACES

For all our family and friends,
For flowers and for food;
For light and laughter and for love,
We give Thee gratitude.

Amen

The bread is on our table
(Bless those who have no bread);
And give us grace in sharing
This bounty round us spread.

Amen

GRACES

Dear God:

Baby is too small to pray
Or thank You in a proper way;
Please bless her pudding and her meat
And everything she tries to eat.

Amen

Be our Guest, Lord Jesus,
At this festive board;
Give us joy in eating;
Be our Guest adored.

Amen

BUYING
HIS OWN

With his father's help, a boy built a model motorboat with a real petrol engine. The boy was very much excited when he took the boat for its trial run. He sailed it for some time on the river that ran near his house. But then, halfway across the stream, the motor stopped, and the little boat was carried downstream.

The boy tried hard to reach his boat, but could not. At last he had to go home without it. To him the boat was lost.

Not long afterwards he and his father went to a nearby town farther down the river. In a shop window, the boy was surprised to see a model motorboat. A sign on it read: THIS BOAT FOR SALE. PRICE TWO POUNDS.
But the boy knew that the boat was the one he had lost. It was *his* boat!

He pulled his father into the shop. "I made that boat," he told the shopkeeper. "See that red line of paint on the back and the little scratch on the side. It's mine. I lost it on the river."

But the shopkeeper would not give it to him. "You can have it for two pounds," he said firmly.

Finally the father answered, "All right, son. We'll buy the boat back."

When the shopkeeper took it from the window, the boy hugged the boat and said, "You are twice mine; I made you, and then I bought you back."

Of course the boat really belonged to the boy. And you see, we belong to God in just the same way. We are His because He made us. Then we are His, too, because He bought us back by sending His Son Jesus into our world to take us by the hand and lead us, each one, back to our Father.

TONGUES
AND TOOTHPASTE

Tommy had been telling his playmates that Jim — the new boy — had cheated in the neighbourhood baseball game. Tommy's father heard the story. Since he had seen the game, he doubted that Jim had cheated.

That night he and Tommy had a man-to-man talk about it. But Tommy didn't seem a bit troubled. He said, "O.K., maybe he didn't cheat. I'll just take back what I said."

"Will you?" his father answered. "You know, son, it isn't as easy as that. Come here with me." And he took Tommy into the bathroom.

There he handed Tommy a fat tube of toothpaste. "Squeeze some out on the basin for me."

Tommy thought that was a queer thing to do. But he squeezed some of the toothpaste out onto the basin in long ribbon-like strips.

"Now, son — put that toothpaste back into the tube."

The little boy obediently tried. First he used the end of his toothbrush; then he tried a toothpick; then, his mother's nail file. But he soon found that there isn't any way to get toothpaste back into a tube.

"You see, Tommy," his father explained. "Your tongue let out a story that wasn't true. And you don't know how many people have heard that story by now. You can't take your words back any more than you can put the toothpaste back."

Tommy hung his head. "Then how can I make it right for Jim?"

"You can't completely undo what you've done. But you can tell God you're sorry, and then ask Jim to forgive you."

"All right," said Tommy, thoughtfully. "But I guess it's really better not to squeeze the tube in the first place."

THERE IS GLADNESS EVERYWHERE

The ships glide in at the harbour's mouth,
And the ships sail out to sea,
And the wind that sweeps from the
    sunny south
Is sweet as sweet can be.
There's a world of toil and a world of pains,
And a world of trouble and care,
But O in a world where our Father reigns,
There is gladness everywhere!

The harvest waves in the breezy morn,
And the men go forth to reap;
The fullness comes to the tasselled corn,
Whether we wake or sleep.
And far on the hills by feet untrod
There are blossoms that scent the air,
For O in this world of our Father, God,
There is beauty everywhere!

MARGARET ELIZABETH SANGSTER

WE THANK THEE

For flowers that bloom about our feet;
For tender grass, so fresh, so sweet;
For song of bird, and hum of bee;
For all things fair we hear or see,
　　　Father in heaven, we thank Thee!

For blue of stream and blue of sky;
For pleasant shade of branches high;
For fragrant air and cooling breeze;
For beauty of the blooming trees,
　　　Father in heaven, we thank Thee!

RALPH WALDO EMERSON

BIG SHOT —
THE LITTLE SUNFISH

A fisherman had placed in a deep dish full of water some fish he had caught in the lake. In the cottage by the side of the lake he began to clean the fish for the frying pan.

One by one he took out the fish and cut them up. And surely you will agree that things looked hopeless for the remaining fish in the dish.

But there was one little fish that had not given up hope. He was determined to get back to the lake. Of course, he didn't know where the lake was, but the first thing to do was to get out of the dish. So he jumped out.

As he flopped around on the floor, the fisherman scooped him up and put him back in the dish — and again he jumped out.

The fisherman was annoyed as he tossed him back again, but he was forced to notice this peppy little fellow who was so different from the others.

Next time the fisherman's hand was dipped into the dish for a fish the plucky one dodged out of reach and escaped. Then he hopped out again.

There was a bucket nearby, a bucket with high sides; so the fisherman dumped the whole lot into it and continued his job. But still, each time the fisherman groped in the bucket, the little fish escaped.

As the number of fish in the tub got down to a half dozen, this fish looked at the high walls of his prison and felt desperate. Worth trying, he thought. Why not? He gathered his strength. ... Out he went.

This, the fisherman decided, would be a good time to clean him. But he just didn't have the heart.

"Get back in there, Big Shot," said the fisherman, and flipped him in.

One by one, the other fish were taken from the dish and cut up. Five, four, three, two — now only Big Shot and one dead companion remained. The little sunfish still didn't give up.

He flitted back and forth and round and round. As his enemy watched, he nosed up and over the side of the bucket with startling suddenness.

The fisherman watched him for a moment. Then he dumped the dead fish into the dustbin, ran some clean water from the tap into the bucket, and put the fighting sunfish back in.

He picked up the bucket and walked down to the lake and dropped the little fish into the water. As the fisherman watched the small sunfish disappear into deep water with a final flip of his tail, he pondered a lesson he had just learned.

We are never beaten until we give up.

Next time you are discouraged, think of Big Shot, the little sunfish!

SOLOMON
AND THE BEES

Solomon was one of the greatest kings of the Jews. He was also one of the wisest men who ever lived.

Once the Queen of Sheba made a long journey to visit Solomon and to see if he was really wise. She brought him many beautiful presents and asked him many hard questions. Solomon answered every question correctly.

But one day the Queen thought of a new way to test his wisdom. She invited Solomon to come to a grand feast in the palace garden. Then she said to him, "King, among these flowers are some that were made by skilled workmen. Tell me, I pray you, which of the flowers are real and which are not?"

Solomon looked at the flowers a long time, but he could see no difference between them. But then he had an idea. He turned to his servants and said, "Bring in a hive of bees."

When the servants came back, the King said, "Now put the bees down among the flowers."

In a moment the bees began flying all over the garden looking for honey. But they flew only to the real flowers, for of course there was no honey in the man-made ones.

When the Queen of Sheba saw this, she bowed low before Solomon. "You are indeed a wise man, O King. You have answered my question."

"Not I," said Solomon smiling, "but my counsellors the bees. Anything that is not real, O Queen, will give itself away sooner or later."

BRADLEY
DOES HIS SUMS

Bradley was a little boy who had begun to think that money could buy anything. He had never stopped to think that gold cannot buy the most important thing in the world — Love.

One morning when Bradley came down to breakfast he put on his mother's plate a little piece of paper neatly folded. His mother opened it. She could hardly believe it, but this is what Bradley had written:

Going to shops — 25 p
taking out rubbish — 10 p
taking old music lesson — 15 p
hanging up things — 5p
total _____ 55p

His mother smiled but did not say anything. When lunchtime came she placed the bill on Bradley's plate with fifty-five pence.

Bradley's eyes fairly danced when he saw the money. "Great, I'm in business," he said. But with the money there was another little bill which read like this:

Bradley owes Mother and Dad:

For being good ———— 00p

For clothes, shoes and toys —— 00p

For meals and his beautiful
                    room —— 00p

For nursing him through his
long illness with scarlet fever —— 00p

Total Bradley owes Mother
              and Dad —— 00p

Tears came into Bradley's eyes. He put his arms around his mother's neck, put his hand with the fifty-five pence into hers, and said, "Take the money all back, Mum, and just let me love you and Dad and help you for nothing."

THE BOY WITH
THE SHINING FACE

In the Far West of America is an Indian village. Rising out of the desert and towering over the village is a high mountain. Only the very strong can climb it, so all the boys of the village were eager to try.

One day the chief said, "Now, boys, today you may try to climb the mountain. Each of you go as far as you can. When you are too tired to go on, come back. But I want each of you to bring me a twig from the place where you turned back."

Very soon a fat boy came puffing back. In his hand he held out to the chief a cactus leaf. The chief smiled. "My boy, you did not even reach the foot of the mountain. Cactus is a desert flower." Later a second boy returned. He carried a twig of sagebrush. "Well," said the chief, "at least you reached the foot of the mountain."

The next boy to come back had in his hand a cottonwood twig. "Good," said the chief. "You climbed as far as the springs." Another boy came back with some buckthorn. "You, my boy, were really climbing. You were up to the first rocks."

An hour afterwards, one boy came back with a branch of pine. To him the chief said, "Good! You made three-quarters of the climb."

The sun was low in the sky when the last boy returned. His hands were empty, but his face was shining. He said, "Father, there were no trees where I was. I saw no twigs, but I saw a shining sea."

Now the old chief's face glowed too. "I knew it! When I looked at your face, I knew it. ... You have been to the top. You needed no twig to tell me. It is written in your eyes. You alone, my boy, have seen the glory and the peace of the mountain."

You know, the very same thing happens to you and me when we have been with our Father in heaven and have talked to Him in prayer and felt His Presence in our hearts. It shows on our faces. It shines in our eyes. We don't have to tell anyone. Other people will see it and know and be glad.

THANKSGIVING
IN REVERSE

Dear God, You know all about me —
even my thoughts.
So I suppose You know there are some
things I'm not thankful for ...
Things like having to wash so often,
especially behind my ears ...
Getting my hair cut and getting
itchy hair down my neck ...
Injections at the doctor's ...
Having to go to bed so early when
exciting things are still happening ...
Waiting such a long time for grownups
when they say, "Presently, dear —."

Having to share my red wagon with that
new little boy ...
The way my baby sister crawls on my
toys and bangs them around and yells
quite a lot ...
Measles — and freckles and warts ...
Flies and mosquitoes (Why did
You make them anyway?)
I suppose grownups
always have things they don't like too.
I suppose it will always be that way.
But I'm just me and I can't seem
to make myself different.
So — dear God, since You made me in
the first place,
I'm sure You can change me.
Will you please help me to put up with
the things I have to put up with?

And help me to be nice to my baby sister and the new little boy?
Thank You, God, for Your help.

Amen

I KNEW
GOD WAS THERE

After my playing was over
I went into our house;
The fire was lit;
The kitchen smelled so nice — like ginger;
I knew my Mother was at home,
Even though I could not see her.

After my breakfast was over
I went outside to play;
The rugs of grass were laid;
The earth smelled so nice — like flowers;
I knew God was there,
Even though I could not see Him.

ELIZABETH ANNE CAMPAGNA

THE LATCHSTRING
WAS OUT

Long ago doors were fastened with a heavy wooden latch. The door could be opened from the outside by a thong made of deerskin. When this latch was pulled inside, no one could open the door. So friendly people used to say, "Come and see me soon. The latchstring is out." That meant that guests were welcome.

Once when the city of Cincinnati was just a frontier fort, the Indians went on the warpath. Most of the settlers grew frightened and rushed inside the fort for safety. But there was one family that stayed on in its log cabin outside the fort. They had come from William Penn's colony in Pennsylvania and were called Friends or Quakers. William Penn had taught them that when the Indians were treated kindly, as God wants all men and women to be treated, they would be peaceful and friendly. Penn had proved that this was right, for back in Pennsylvania there were no Indian wars. So the family in the cabin decided to try Penn's way. They did not even have any guns ready.

But one night the man grew a bit frightened and put the latchstring on the inside. He and his wife could not go to sleep. Finally she said, "John, that latchstring on the inside makes me feel uneasy."

"I feel that way too, Mary," he replied. So he got up and put the latchstring outside again.

Before long they heard the Indians coming. Soon they surrounded the little cabin with wild cries and war whoops. They tried the door and saw that it would open, but did not come in. Then, after a while, they grew quiet and began to steal away. Mary and John crept on hands and knees to a window and watched them. On the edge of the forest, the Indians sat down in a circle. They seemed to be holding a council to talk things over.

"What do you suppose they're going to do?" Mary whispered.

"Sh-h-h," said John. "Remember God has promised us, 'I will never leave thee or forsake thee.'"

But soon they saw a tall chieftain in war paint leave the circle. Slowly he walked back to the cabin alone. In his right hand he carried a long white feather. He fastened the feather to the top of the cabin door. Then all the Indians left.

There the white feather stayed for a long time. The hot summer sun shone on it. It swayed in the winter winds that swept the prairie. John and Mary never took it down. For a friendly Indian told them: "The white feather means: 'This is the home of a man of peace. Do not harm him.'"

All this happened long ago. But God has not changed. He still wants us to be kind and fair to all men, and then to trust Him to take care of us.

HOW TO GET THE BEST OF A BURGLAR

Jesus told us to do some things which seem strange. For example, He said that when a man wants to take away our coat, we should not only let him have it and not fight back, but we should also give him our cloak (Matthew 5:40).

Why do you suppose Jesus said that? He was very wise. He knew that when we fight back, we just make more trouble for ourselves. But when we do not fight back, then He can help us.

When something we say or do surprises another person, we say they are "disarmed". Jesus' way is sometimes really disarming.

I know a man who did exactly what Jesus said. His name was Brother Bryan. He was a minister who lived in Birmingham, Alabama.

One Thursday night Brother Bryan had stayed late at his church and was walking home alone. As he crossed a narrow, dark alley, a man stuck a gun in his ribs and said, "Stick 'em up."

Brother Bryan obediently put up his hands, and the thief searched through his pockets and took his watch and some money.

"Brother," said the minister, "you've missed some. There's a little more money in the other pocket."Then, as the thief reached for that too, he was astonished to hear his victim say, "Brother, let us pray." And the minister did pray. His prayer had a surprising effect. The thief hurriedly thrust all the money and the watch back into Brother Bryan's hands and rushed away without a single thing. Jesus' way had worked!

PICTURE
OF PEACE

There was once a king who offered a prize
to the artist who would paint the best picture of peace. Many artists tried. The king
looked at all the pictures. But there were
only two that he really liked, and he had to
choose between them.

One picture was of a calm lake. The lake was a perfect mirror for peaceful towering mountains all around it. Overhead was a blue sky with fluffy white clouds. All who saw this picture thought that it was a perfect picture of peace.

The other picture had mountains too. But these were rugged and bare. Above was an angry sky, from which rain fell and in which lightning played. Down the side of the mountain tumbled a foaming waterfall. This did not look peaceful at all.

But when the king looked closely, he saw behind the waterfall a tiny bush growing in a crack in the rock. In the bush a mother bird had built her nest. There, in the midst of the rush of angry water, in the wind and the noise, sat the mother bird on her nest — in perfect peace.

Which picture do you think won the prize? The king chose the second picture. Do you know why?

"Because," explained the king, "peace does not mean to be in a place where there is no noise, trouble, or hard work.

Peace means to be in the midst of all those things and still be calm in your heart. That is the real meaning of peace."

LITTLE DOG LOST

Dear Jesus, this is Johnny again ...
My dog Jeff is lost, and I need Your help;
I had him for his evening walk;
He broke away to chase a squirrel —
Before I could catch him,
    he was out of sight,
Mum and Dad and I have searched
    everywhere ...
And how can I enjoy my warm bed tonight
with Jeffey in the cold?
(He can't chase squirrels all night!)
So, dear Jesus, will You please
    take care of Jeff
and lead him safely home?
Thank You for this special help.

Amen

LITTLE DOG FOUND

Thank You, Jesus —
     Jeffey's home again...
He woke me up this morning
scratching on the front door;
He was *so* tired and hungry
with what tail he has between his legs.
I think he'd like to say he's sorry...
It's true, he's been a bad dog lately,
chewing up newspapers and jumping
     on furniture;
But sometimes I've been bad too
and still You love me just the same...
So, dear Jesus, will You love Jeff
     into being good
and help him not to run away again?
Thank you.

Amen

BIRTHDAY WISH

Jesus, when You were six like me,
Was six a lovely age to be?
And did You stand up straight and tall
For birthday measures on the wall?
Did You have candles on *Your* cake,
A special birthday wish to make?
Please bless all children on their Day
And make them happy in their play.

ELIZABETH ANNE CAMPAGNA

THE BIRDS' CHRISTMAS TREE

It was Christmas Eve. Outside, the snow was falling in big downy flakes. When we picked up the evening paper from our front steps, we found it almost covered with snow. On the front page was this little notice:

ATTENTION: BIRD LOVERS

This is proving to be a hard winter for the birds in this area to find food. Why not remember the birds too at Christmas time?

I read the notice to Peter John. "I know!" he said excitedly. "Why can't we have a Christmas tree for the birds?"
Peter-daddy and I agreed that this would be a fine idea.
"Let's put it on the porch of my bird-house," Peter John said. This was a house he had made at school. It was mounted on a pole in the back yard, and the whole family was proud of it.
We decorated the birds' tree with bits of coloured yarn, some tiny popcorn balls, and some cranberries strung together.

Then we tied things on the branches that the birds would like: small doughnuts; some empty walnut shells filled with raisins, cracked corn, and sunflower seeds; others filled with peanut butter. We packed some soft suet into pine cones and fastened the cones to the tree.

Then we hid inside the house and watched out of the windows to see what would happen. In no time at all a jay, a blue tit, and three sparrows were enjoying a feast. Then came a song thrush and a pair of robins. One of the robins stopped eating long enough to sit on top of the birdhouse and sing awhile. Since he was the right Christmas colour, we thought he must surely be singing a bird's carol. Anyway, he seemed to be saying in his own way, "Thank you for remembering God's small creatures at Christmas time."

THE TOY DOG

"Hurry, Caspar." It was the eldest of the Wise Men of the East who spoke. "Why do you delay? The camels are ready; the way is long. We must get started."

But still Caspar — the youngest of the Wise Men — delayed. Rich gifts for the newborn Babe, the King of Kings, were already laden upon the patient camels — sacks filled with gold, frankincense, and myrrh. A brilliant star stood in a sapphire sky, waiting to point the way. But still Caspar lingered.

When the others asked him why he delayed, the young king could not tell. The camels, in their crimson and gold trappings, finally grew restless, and swayed and snarled. Purple shadows lengthened across the cooling sands of the desert. Still Caspar sat and thought deeply.

At length, he smiled and rose. Hurriedly, he mounted to a high-vaulted chamber at the top of his palace. This was the room in which he had played as a child. He rummaged about, and after a while came out, bearing something in his hand.

The Wise Men thought that Caspar surely bore some new gift, more rare and precious than all the riches they had been able to find in their treasure rooms. But in Caspar's hand was a toy. It was a cuddly dog, its soft white fur a little soiled.

Still smiling, the young king pressed his fingers to the dog's sides, and lo, it barked! A child, the son of one of the camel drivers, laughed and clapped his hands. But the older Wise Men looked stern and disapproving.

"What folly has seized you, Caspar?" cried the eldest. "Is that a gift fit for the King of Kings?"

But Caspar replied gently, "For the King of Kings, we have all these rare and costly treasures. But this — this toy dog — is a birthday gift for the Child of Bethlehem."

FOLLOW
THE LEADER

The Morris family had been on a picnic.
As they got in their car to start home,
Patty Morris asked, "What's that, Dad?"
pointing to a swirling mist in the air.

"That's fog," her father answered. "And
it's hard to drive in."

He drove very slowly, but could scarcely
see through the fog enough to stay on the
road. Suddenly another car, going much
faster, passed him.

"That man seems to know where he's
going," Mr. Morris said. "I think I'll just
follow his red tail lights."

So they drove along that way for a while,
until all at once the red tail lights ahead
disappeared. Then — Wham! There was a
loud crash. Patty was jolted a bit, but no
one was hurt. This is what had happened:
they had followed the man in the car
ahead right into his own garage and had
knocked his car smack through the back
garage wall.

Mr. Morris stood looking at the splintered
garage wall and the dented cars and said
sadly, "Well, Patty, I suppose it isn't safe

to follow people unless you know where they are going."

He was right. There is really only one Leader whom you can safely follow, and that Leader is Jesus Christ. Let Him lead you, and everything will be all right.

Beyond Ourselves

Catherine Marshall

A memorable spiritual autobiography

'If you are satisfied with your life and feel no need for any help outside yourself, this book is not for you. The search for God begins at the point of need.'

Catherine Marshall brings compelling enthusiasm and insight to her exploration of the Christian faith. *Beyond Ourselves* will answer the needs of anyone searching for a more direct relationship with God. In describing her own faith Catherine Marshall ranges over an appealing variety of subjects — childhood, early college days, friends who helped and inspired her, the moving death of her minister father, the work and influence of Peter Marshall. Here is wisdom and truth, as well as a portrait of an extraordinary woman.

Meeting God at Every Turn

Catherine Marshall

A moving account of God's faithfulness and loving instruction

'I have met God at moments when the straight road turns. He has picked me up, wiped away the tears, and set me back on the path of life.'

On her wedding day, Catherine Marshall's daughter Linda made a special request: that Catherine should sum up what she had learned about God, and his plan for life and families. In *Meeting God at Every Turn*, she has selected 'twelve key periods in my life where an encounter with the Lord has come at a turning point or during a moment of crisis.' Catherine's own story is told with unsurpassed detail and intimacy, revealing God's gracious dealings with her and her family.

'A book that never runs away from realities . . . it is religion touching life for enrichment and renewal at every point.'

Methodist Recorder

Adventures in Prayer

Catherine Marshall

How prayer works: a thrilling and inspiring account

With compassion and honesty, Catherine Marshall shares incidents in her own life and the lives of others which confirm the truth: God does hear and answer prayer.

'Eight types of personal prayer are considered: asking, helplessness, dreams, waiting, relinquishment, secret, joyous blessing and claiming. From the impoverished young man with the impossible dream of going to college, to George Müller who financed orphanages through secret prayer, to Catherine herself who, helplessly ill, is healed as a result of prayer, the true stories told in this book are a powerful testimony to the power of prayer.

'Mrs Marshall writes directly and with charm . . . the chapters breathe generally the stuff of life.'
Church Times